CH

1999
The first popular smartphones are released, making the Internet available to people on the move.

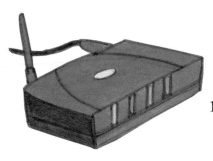

2005
Google Earth provides free, scalable mapping of the whole world over the Internet.

1989
Tim Berners-Lee proposes the World Wide Web.

1993
Web browser Mosaic brings the Web to everyone.

2014
A wrench is 3D-printed on the International Space Station, using a file e-mailed from Earth.

1977
The Apple II becomes the first mass-market personal computer.

2004
Approximate start of Web 2.0, which lets ~~build their own~~

Internet Use Around the World

Percentage of people with Internet access on each continent.

Lowest   *Highest*

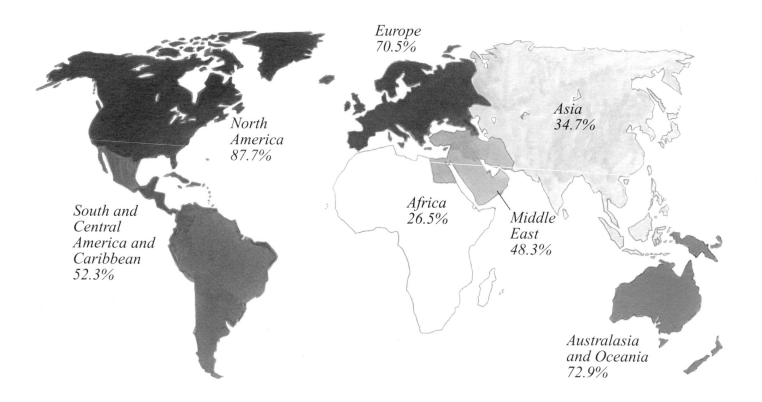

Europe
70.5%

Asia
34.7%

North America
87.7%

Africa
26.5%

Middle East
48.3%

South and Central America and Caribbean
52.3%

Australasia and Oceania
72.9%

How many people use the Internet where you live?

In Asia, 1.386 billion people use the Internet. But that's only a third (34.7%) of Asia's huge population.

In North America, 87.7% of the population uses the Internet, or 310 million people.

In Europe, 70.5% of the population (nearly three people out of four) uses the Internet; that comes to 582 million people.

In Australasia and Oceania, 72.9% of people (26.8 million) use the Internet. The Middle East has 112 million users. South and Central America, including the Caribbean, have 320 million between them.

The lowest level of Internet use is in Africa, where only one in four people has access to the Internet. That's 26.5% of the population, or 298 million people.

(Figures correct as of 2014)

Author:

Anne Rooney studied English at Cambridge University, England, and then earned a Ph.D. at Cambridge. She has held teaching posts at several UK universities and is currently a Royal Literary Fund fellow at Newnham College, Cambridge. She has written more than 150 books for children and adults, including several on the history of science and medicine. She also writes children's fiction.

Artist:

Mark Bergin was born in Hastings, England, in 1961. He studied at Eastbourne College of Art and has specialized in historical reconstructions as well as aviation and maritime subjects since 1983. He lives in Bexhill-on-Sea, England, with his wife and three children.

Series creator:

David Salariya was born in Dundee, Scotland. He has illustrated a wide range of books and has created and designed many new series for publishers in the UK and overseas. David established The Salariya Book Company in 1989. He lives in Brighton, England, with his wife, illustrator Shirley Willis, and their son, Jonathan.

Editor: **Stephen Haynes**

Editorial Assistants: **Mark Williams, Rob Walker**

Cover artwork: **David Antram**

© The Salariya Book Company Ltd MMXVI

No part of this publication may be reproduced in whole or in part, or stored in a retrieval system, or transmitted in any form or by any means, electronic, mechanical, photocopying, recording, or otherwise, without written permission of the publisher. For information regarding permission, write to the copyright holder.

Published in Great Britain in 2016 by
The Salariya Book Company Ltd
25 Marlborough Place, Brighton BN1 1UB

ISBN-13: 978-0-531-21931-7 (lib. bdg.) 978-0-531-22055-9 (pbk.)

All rights reserved.
Published in 2016 in the United States
by Franklin Watts
An imprint of Scholastic Inc.
Published simultaneously in Canada.

A CIP catalog record for this book is available from the Library of Congress.

Printed and bound in China.
Printed on paper from sustainable sources.

1 2 3 4 5 6 7 8 9 10 R 25 24 23 22 21 20 19 18 17 16

SCHOLASTIC, FRANKLIN WATTS, and associated logos are trademarks and/or registered trademarks of Scholastic Inc.

PAPER FROM
SUSTAINABLE
FORESTS

You Wouldn't Want to Live Without the
Internet!™

Written by
Anne Rooney

Illustrated by
Mark Bergin

Series created by
David Salariya

Franklin Watts®
An Imprint of Scholastic Inc.

Contents

Introduction

Where do you go if you want to know what an aardvark looks like, how to make a kaleidoscope, or which planet or moon is most likely to be home to aliens? Probably online!

Over the last 20 years the Internet—and especially the World Wide Web—has become the first place we look for information. And we don't head online just to find things out. We watch videos, catch up on TV shows, keep in touch, go shopping, hang out with friends, show off our photos, and a host of other things. We're online from our computers, laptops, tablets, phones, and even watches. Could you live without the Internet? Would you want to? Do you dare try?

Online Safety

Before you go online, read page 33 for tips on how to stay safe.

Don't worry, you can still use books!

What Exactly Is the Internet?

The Internet and the Web—what's the difference? It's easy to mix them up.

The Internet is a physical network of connected computers; the Web is a vast set of linked files kept on those computers. As we share, copy, view, and move information, the network buzzes with activity. It's never off, never quiet—and sometimes parts of it are so overloaded that everything slows down, like a massive data traffic jam.

The Internet isn't home only to the Web. Data of all kinds move around over the Internet. Every time you send an e-mail or an instant message, store a file in cloud storage, or play an online game on your console, you're using the Internet.

Movie theater (online video)

Street-corner speaker (blog)

Bookstore (e-book store)

TO MOVE around the Internet, information is changed to strings of numbers. It's changed back to meaningful information by the computer at the other end—you never see the numbers.

JUST LIKE a traffic highway, the Internet has a choice of different routes to every place. Sometimes it's super-busy!

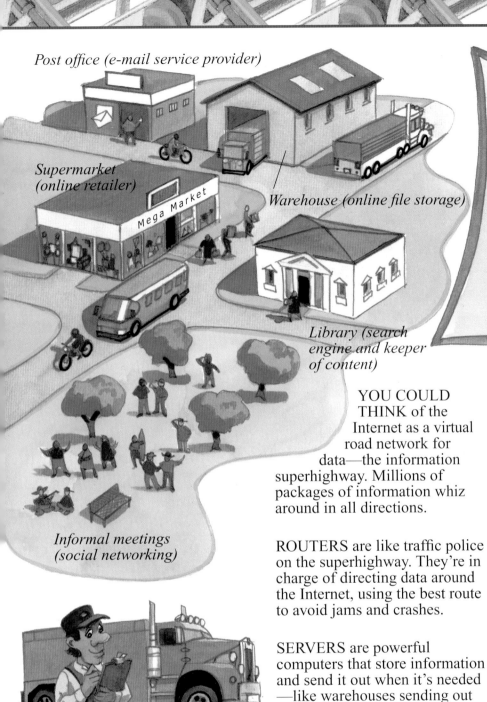

Post office (e-mail service provider)

Supermarket (online retailer)

Mega Market

Warehouse (online file storage)

Library (search engine and keeper of content)

Informal meetings (social networking)

The Internet links computers using wires and radio waves. At home, you have a modem that plugs into the cable network that runs underground. Your phone, tablet, and other items communicate with the modem wirelessly, using radio waves.

YOU COULD THINK of the Internet as a virtual road network for data—the information superhighway. Millions of packages of information whiz around in all directions.

ROUTERS are like traffic police on the superhighway. They're in charge of directing data around the Internet, using the best route to avoid jams and crashes.

SERVERS are powerful computers that store information and send it out when it's needed —like warehouses sending out goods that people have ordered.

FILES are split up and sent in chunks, then put back together at the other end. It's like breaking up a jigsaw puzzle and mailing the parts separately to a friend.

What Can You Do on the Internet?

You can use the Internet almost anywhere, from the top of a mountain to a ship in the middle of the ocean—as long as you have one of the billions of Internet-enabled devices in the world.

We've all grown dependent on the Internet very quickly. We rely on it for entertainment, communication, shopping, banking, health care, news, government—all the things that keep our societies running smoothly. In fact, it's more a question of what *can't* you do on the Internet!

YOU CAN BUY almost anything online, from a meteorite to a tiger (check with a parent first). Most people settle for books, games, clothes, food, and music.

Amazing! Something for everyone!

You Can Do It!

How many Internet-connected devices do you have at home? Computer, laptop, tablet, phone, game console? Make a list. What do you use them all for? Do you use each one differently?

WHAT DO YOU LIKE to watch or listen to? Whatever you like, you'll find it somewhere online. Baby sloths playing? There's a Webcam for that. Mongolian throat singing? No problem. Missed your favorite TV show last week? The Internet is your time machine!

YOU CAN PLAY online games on your own, with friends down the road, or even with people on the other side of the world.

IF YOU WANT to learn something your school doesn't teach—like Aleut or guitar-playing —there will be lessons online. Or you can go online for help with your homework.

Hi, Gramps!

YOU CAN CHAT to friends and family anywhere in the world online. Or use blogging and microblogging sites to share your interests with everyone.

DOES NO ONE BELIEVE your dog can skateboard? Post a video on a social media or file-sharing page and they can see it for themselves!

9

How Did We Share Information Before?

The world wasn't an information vacuum before the Internet. People have been talking for thousands of years. Then we started writing—that made it possible to communicate with someone who wasn't right there with you. Printing made that even easier. Then we developed radio and television and it was possible to see and hear someone far away. We can even watch live videos from space and other planets now—communications have come a long way.

READING really took off after Johannes Gutenberg made the first European printing press, around 1450. Suddenly, books were everywhere.

Screw for pressing down the platen

Compositors assembling the type

Printer removing printed pages

Printer inking the type

Platen

THE EARLIEST WRITING was pressed into clay tablets with a special stick called a stylus. That was in ancient Sumer more than 5,000 years ago. And now we've gone right back to writing on tablets with a stylus!

Top Tip

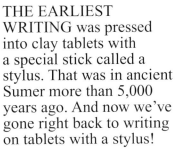

Don't neglect the old methods of communication—they still work! Add the Internet as well, but keep reading books, writing, and talking to people face-to-face.

FOR CENTURIES, people wrote with a quill pen that had to be dipped into ink every few words. It took a long time to write out a whole book.

RADIO (below left) was invented in 1866, but at first it was only used for Morse code—letters coded in dots and dashes. The first voice broadcast was in 1906, in Massachusetts.

TELEVISION has been around only since the 1920s, and it was only in black and white at first.

THE FIRST MOVABLE TYPE was made in China about 1,000 years ago. Chinese writing has thousands of characters. Printers used a separate wooden block for each one.

The Geeks Are Coming!

Imagine how long it would take if you had to do every calculation by hand. That's why people invented automatic calculating machines. But having to tell the machine exactly what to do each time was a bore. How could this be improved? The answer was programming—preparing a list of instructions for the machine to follow and letting it do the job itself.

The first modern programmable machine was a loom for weaving patterns into fabric. Now, lots of machines—including looms—can do things on their own, controlled by computers and programming.

THERE HAVE ALWAYS BEEN teenage geeks. Blaise Pascal was only 19 when he started work on the first mechanical calculator, called the Pascaline, in 1642.

CHARLES BABBAGE had bigger ideas. He designed the first programmable computer, or Difference Engine, in the 1820s. Sadly, he couldn't raise the money to build it. A working Difference Engine was constructed in 2002 at London's Science Museum. The Difference Engine is mechanical—it does not use electricity.

It's amazingly accurate.

"Chain" of punched cards

IN 1801, the Jacquard loom followed programs coded as holes punched in cardboard. Early electronic computers did the same.

How It Works

A program is a long list of instructions for a computer to follow. A Web browser has around 50 million instructions —it would fill 900,000 pages if you printed it out.

Uh-oh!

CODEBREAKING goes back to the start of computing. The first programmable electronic digital computer that was actually built was Colossus (right), made at Bletchley Park, England, to crack German codes during World War II.

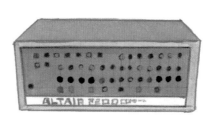

ONE OF THE EARLIEST personal computers was the Altair 8800, designed in 1974. It had no screen, keyboard, or mouse—just lights and switches.

A MOUSE and a desktop are now the standard way of using a computer. They first appeared on a computer called the Lisa in 1983.

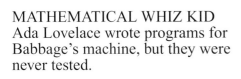

MATHEMATICAL WHIZ KID Ada Lovelace wrote programs for Babbage's machine, but they were never tested.

Where Did the Internet Come From?

Everything starts small. The Internet began in 1969 as ARPAnet, linking just four American universities. It was used to share research, and would provide an emergency means of communication if a war or a natural disaster wiped out other methods.

It grew slowly at first, with all the linked computers in universities or research laboratories on little local networks. Because it linked these separate networks into a single interconnected network, it became known as the Internet.

Now it spans the world and even reaches out into space!

E-MAIL was first used in 1971, and really took off: By 1973, 75% of ARPAnet traffic was e-mail. Now we send about 206 billion e-mails every day—and around 75% of that is junk mail.

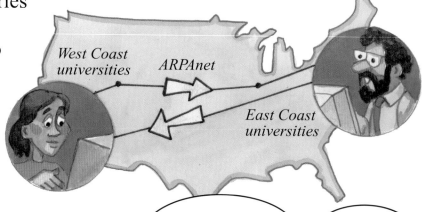
West Coast universities
ARPAnet
East Coast universities

WHAT DO YOU DO on a snow day? In 1978, Ward Christensen spent his snow day building CBBS, a bulletin-board system that let people post messages online.

BLOGS and social networking started in 1980 with Usenet, a news-sharing system that allows groups of members to post themed threads of messages.

Coffee's ready — let's go!
Sure!
WEBCAMS are great for watching playing pandas or roaming rovers on Mars. The very first Webcam was aimed at a coffee pot at Cambridge University, England.

GETTING AHEAD. British queen Elizabeth II became the first national leader to send an e-mail, in 1976.

LATE NIGHT gaming isn't new. The first games were text-only adventures, often involving knights, warriors, and dragons (and a lot of typing).

ASTRONAUT John Glenn spent his 77th birthday on the space shuttle *Discovery*. U.S. president Bill Clinton sent him a "Happy Birthday" e-mail into space.

IMAGINE if you had to keep your tablet and phone plugged in! Luckily, they use radio waves to connect. Early computers, however, all used cables.

Weaving the Web

The World Wide Web is central to our lives today—but it almost didn't happen!

It was invented by British scientist Tim Berners-Lee, who was working at CERN in Switzerland and wanted to share files easily with his colleagues around the world. In 1989, he came up with an idea for linked pages of information kept on different networked computers, and asked if he could develop it. His boss wasn't interested. He said Berners-Lee could do it in his own time, but that it wasn't worth CERN taking on, because his idea was too vague.

WEB PAGES are pretty useless if you can't look at them. Berners-Lee made a browser to display his Web pages at CERN. The browser that made the Web popular with the public was Mosaic, invented by Marc Andreessen and his team and released in 1993.

Interesting but vague.

You Can Do It!

As a child, Tim Berners-Lee made toy computers from old boxes. Make your own fantasy computer from cardboard. What will it be able to do?

THE VERY FIRST Web page, in 1991, wasn't very exciting (above): no dancing pandas then. It was just a list of text links to all the other 25 Web pages. There are now nearly 1 billion pages on the Web.

FINDING FAVORITE BANDS online is as old as the Web. The very first photo on a Web page was of the girl band Les Horribles Cernettes. It was posted in 1992.

THE FIRST SEARCH ENGINE appeared in 1994. Before that there were lists and directories. But it was like looking for a single page in a vast library!

Web 2.0: It's a Two-Way Thing

At first, the Web worked in one direction, like TV and radio: Professionals put information and pictures and videos on the Web, and we could look at it. But now everyone can join in. The Web has become more interactive. It's called Web 2.0 and it lets us all upload and share files and photos. You can write a blog, share your videos, add to a wiki article, comment on a news story, or even make your own Web site. *See page 33 for tips about staying safe while online.*

EVERYONE'S a TV station! If you see something amazing, you can share it immediately by uploading a picture or a video. And if you can't get to the South Pole yourself, at least you can enjoy the amazing things that other people have posted.

And it's all happening right now!

18

WEB 2.0 is open to everyone. People who live far from cities can now follow important issues and take part in international debates. It helps give power to ordinary people!

You Can Do It!

What are you really, really interested in? Dolphins? Music? Cars? Search online—and go beyond the first page of results to find some super sites, groups, and blogs to follow.

SOCIAL NETWORKING means you can keep up with what your friends are doing no matter where they—or you—live.

WANT TO BE a dancer or a musician? Start now! Film your talented self and start your career as an online star.

EVEN the oddest hobbies have a home online. The whole world's out there—you can find other people who like what you like.

IF YOU NEED INFORMATION about an important issue, you can find it online on safe, reliable sites.

19

Information Overload!

ou can find out about anything on the Web, as long as you know how to look for it. It's like the best library in the history of the world, it's free, you don't need a library card, and it's in your own home (or phone!). The catch is that *anyone* can put information online. Some of it is really valuable, and some is total garbage—it can even be dangerously wrong.

THE WEB keeps growing all the time. By 2010, we were adding as much information to the Web every two days as was added in all of 2002. You can never keep up with it all, so you need really good search skills to find what you need.

WHATEVER you want to know, someone will have made a Web site about it. With pictures and videos, it's easy to follow instructions. And you can replay them again and again.

How It Works

Programs called robotic spiders "crawl" the Web gathering information about what's on different Web pages. This is built into a vast index—and that's where a search engine looks when you search.

ALIEN INVASION? You'll find out on the Web first. News spreads superfast online and can be updated instantly.

CITIZEN JOURNALISTS are ordinary people reporting online about big events (right). You can do it yourself! Now we've got everything covered.

> Definitely something wrong with this recipe!

COMMON SENSE. If the information doesn't *look* right, don't trust it! Check other sources to see if they agree.

EVEN if you live miles from anywhere (below), the Web can be a vast school at your fingertips!

21

It's a Virtual World

There's a whole other world (or even many worlds) inside the World Wide Web—a virtual world. You can immerse yourself in games set in imaginary realms, and learn (safely!) in a virtual environment. In real life you can't just cut people up to see what's inside, learn to fly a plane, rule an empire in ancient Egypt, or run your own island. But you can do them all online.

And it's not just fun and games. Pilots can practice landing at real airports thousands of miles away, and surgeons can operate on real patients through a computer screen and a robot.

Now, let's see what's inside here...

VIRTUAL CURRENCIES let you pay online—often for virtual goods, like food for your monster pet.

LEARN real skills in a virtual world. Trainee doctors can now explore the inside of a human body without cutting it up.

Remember there's a real world out there, too! Take a break from playing and learning in the virtual world to get outside and move around. It's good for you!

FLYING a virtual plane is the next best thing to flying a real one. You can learn all the skills of piloting without risking any lives. Even real pilots learn in flight simulators (left) before they fly real passenger planes.

Time to take a break!

ROBOTIC SURGERY machines can be controlled by real surgeons from near or far—useful for accidents at sea or in space.

KEEP YOUR COOL. Virtual mishaps can make you really angry. Too many violent computer games might be bad for you.

Sharing Whether You Want to or Not

The Internet began because researchers wanted to share information. Now we can—and do—share almost everything. We share what we're doing on social networks, and we share our photos and videos. Lots of information about us is kept online by health care providers, schools, and governments, and shared with others who need it. Someone is always keeping an eye on us. Has it gone too far?

Sharing is good—but not *too* much sharing. We need privacy as well. You've probably done things you wouldn't want to share. Who owns information about you, and who's allowed to see it?

SHARING photos with friends and family is great. Make sure you understand privacy settings to keep your pictures secure.

IF YOU HAVE an accident, the Internet allows paramedics to check health information on the spot. It could save your life.

BE CAREFUL about what you post online. Don't give away clues to where you live or go to school, in either text or photos. Protect yourself online to protect yourself in the real world.

ONCE THAT PHOTO of you in your jellyfish hat is online, you can't take it off if it gets shared—so be careful what you share. Never post photos of others without their permission. What looks like a laugh to you might not seem funny to another person.

Top Tip

There are lots of free music tracks, movies, and books online, but some are pirated (stolen and posted without the creator's permission). Not only is it illegal to download these, it's unfair to steal someone's work.

THE WEB remembers what you look at and shares it with advertisers. You may be bombarded with ads for things you might like—but also for some things you don't like or already have.

SHARING online is a good way to show people what you can do. Some bands give away tracks to advertise their real-world gigs.

WHO'S LOOKING?
Governments monitor online activity. They say it helps fight crime and keep us all safe. But some people are concerned about the invasion of their privacy.

THERE'S ANOTHER good reason not to download pirated content: Illegal downloads often contain viruses that may damage your files or your computer.

25

A Global Village

It's been called a "wired world" and the "global village." The Internet connects people everywhere, shrinking the world so that we're all neighbors. You can see the weather on a beach in Australia while you sit in your bedroom in Europe or the United States. Someone in China can chat with a friend in Peru. You can campaign to save rhinos or supply water to a remote village. It's as easy to see something on the other side of the world as something outside your window. The Internet can bring us all closer.

SEEING how other people live can give us greater understanding of other cultures and make us more tolerant. We're less likely to believe propaganda about other groups if we see and interact with those people online. It's hard to hate someone you've compared fish photos with.

Many Amazonian Indians have access to the Internet.

That's bigger than the one you caught.

NOW THAT EVERYONE can upload photos, it's hard to keep things secret, including the bad things that happen in some places. Here's to a fairer, safer world!

You Can Do It!

Find an online campaign for a cause you care about, and do something to support it. If there isn't one, start your own. You can make a difference!

ORDINARY people everywhere share their experiences. If there's no TV camera around, it doesn't matter—there will be someone with a smartphone (below).

Have you looked online?

We don't have a computer.

AS MORE THINGS happen online, people without the Internet lose out. It's harder to get information and take part in what's going on in the world.

SELLERS give online discounts, so people who don't have access to the Internet may miss out on the best deals and end up paying more for things.

THE INTERNET means campaigns can be global. People on the other side of the world can help causes they would never have heard of before the Internet.

50% off!

So, Would You Want to Live Without the Internet?

If the Internet were turned off tomorrow, the world would fall into chaos—banking, emergency services, health care, education, entertainment, and even getting food into stores all depend on the Internet now. Yet only 40 years ago, it was used by just a few people for business and research.

The next big thing is likely to be the "Internet of things" (IoT), in which more and more ordinary devices are connected to the Internet. Examples might include automobiles, home thermostats, and security systems. Industry experts predict there could be 50 billion things of all types online by 2020. With the Internet running everything, we really wouldn't want to live without it!

Welcome home! Your dinner is ready. ♥

HOW ABOUT a refrigerator that orders food when you run out? Could the future see kitchens that never run out of milk, and the end of physical supermarkets?

WEARABLE COMPUTERS can upload information about your activity and state of health. Are they just gadgets for fitness fanatics, or could they catch on?

You Can Do It!

Have a totally offline day—a digital detox! No Web sites, no online games, videos, or TV, no social networking... Dare we ask—how did it go?

WIRED houses can pretty much run themselves. They can turn on the heating when you're on your way home, and turn the lights off when you go out. It's not just fun —it saves energy, so it's good for the planet, too.

Access denied

SOME people have to live without the Internet. In some countries, where leaders don't want their citizens to see how people live elsewhere, it's banned.

THE INTERNET extends into space now. The Deep Space Network communicates with faraway spacecraft. Some craft even have their own social networking pages!

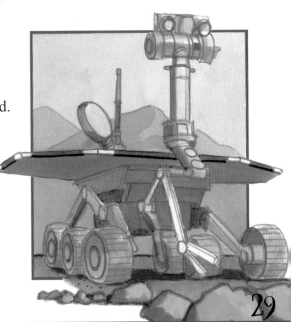

Glossary

ARPAnet The early network of computers in the United States that later developed into the Internet.

Browser A program for displaying and interacting with Web pages.

Bulletin board (or **Web forum**) A Web site that allows people to post and respond to notices or news items in threads (themed discussions).

CERN European Organization for Nuclear Research (Geneva, Switzerland).

Cloud storage Keeping files on a remote server connected to the Internet, instead of a hard disk or local network drive.

Data Raw information, including facts, figures, pictures, sound, or video.

File A document stored on a computer, such as a text document, picture, spreadsheet, or video clip.

Internet-enabled device Any device that can access the Internet, including computers, smartphones, and Webcams.

Microblog A blogging platform that allows only very short updates, often less than 200 characters.

Modem A device that connects a computer (or a wireless network) to the Internet.

Monitor (verb) To keep watch over or keep track of something.

Movable type An old printing technology in which each character is printed from a separate small block of metal or wood. Once the page has been printed, the type can be taken apart, reassembled, and used to print something else.

Online Connected to or available on the Internet.

Paramedic A health care professional who specializes in immediate care in an emergency.

Platen The flat plate in a printing press that presses the paper against the inked printing block.

Program A set of instructions written in computer code that tells a computer what to do. Some programs are very long and complicated, such as image-processing programs and Web browsers.

Propaganda Biased information that is presented in a way intended to persuade people, or win them over to a particular point of view.

Quill pen A pen made from the central tube (quill) of a feather.

Search engine A Web site that keeps a very complex and full database of words that appear on Web pages and allows you to search through this to find Web pages about a particular topic.

Social networking The use of social media sites to keep in touch with and share files with a large number of people, usually for fun rather than business.

Sumer A place in the Middle East that was the site of the earliest known civilization. It lies between two rivers, the Tigris and Euphrates, and is now part of southern Iraq.

3D printing Building a physical object in plastic or another material from a file sent from a computer to a 3D printer.

Virtual Not real; simulated by a computer so as to seem realistic.

Virus A program that is deliberately introduced into a computer or network to steal information or to prevent it from working properly.

Wearable computer A piece of clothing or an accessory, such as a watch or wristband, that contains computer technology and can (usually) connect to the Internet.

Webcam A video or still camera that is connected to the Internet and feeds its images to a Web page where people can view them as they occur.

Wiki A publicly sourced collection of information that builds into an online encyclopedia that anyone can use and add to.

Index

Top Ways to Stay Safe Online

You can have a lot of fun on the Internet, but it also has its dangers. Keep yourself safe online by following these guidelines.

- When online, never reveal your real-world contact details, such as your full name, where you live, or which school you go to.

- If anyone says anything to you online that you don't like, or if you see anything that makes you feel uncomfortable, tell a grown-up you can trust, such as a parent or a teacher.

- Don't post anything you might regret later, such as embarrassing photos or stories of stupid things you've done. Information spreads and hangs around for years online.

- Never post anything mean or embarrassing about anyone else— that's cyberbullying.

- Log out of all your accounts and pages before leaving the computer, so that other people can't use them as if they were you.

- Choose passwords that other people can't guess, and don't write them down where they can be seen.

- Never agree to meet up with someone you know only online. Tell a grown-up if someone you know online asks to meet you. Remember that you don't really know who they are—it's easy to pretend online to be someone you're not.

Crazy Internet Statistics

- There are nearly a billion active Web sites on the Web.

- There are around 10 billion Internet-connected devices (computers, tablets, phones, and so on), but only 3 billion or so people in the world who use the Internet.

- Over 26,000 GB (gigabytes) of data are sent over the Internet every second.

- That mass of data includes 2.4 million e-mails sent every second, and most of that is "spam" (junk e-mail).

- One popular search engine hosts 173 million searches every hour.

- Internet "rush hour" is between 7:00 p.m. and 9:00 p.m. in many countries. That's when people are home from work and school and have time to go online.

- 800 million Internet users speak English, and around 700 million speak Chinese. The next most common online languages are Spanish and Arabic, with 136 million each.

- The Internet changes so fast that some of the information on this page is bound to be out of date by the time you read it.